Black Empowerment Journal:

A Reflective Guide for Leaders, Educators and Advocates

Peter E. Carter and
Dr. Elizabeth A. Carter

Copyright © 2025 Dr. Elizabeth A. Carter & Peter E. Carter

All rights reserved. No part of this publication may be reproduced, distributed, or transmitted in any form or by any means, including photocopying, recording, or other electronic or mechanical methods, without the prior written permission of the publisher, except in the case of brief quotations embodied in critical reviews and certain other noncommercial uses permitted by copyright law. For permission requests, write to the publisher, AAPPEAL, LLC, addressed "Attention: Permissions Coordinator," at elizabeth@eac-aappeal.com

Disclaimer: The author has made every effort to ensure the accuracy of the information within this book was correct at time of publication. The author does not assume and hereby denies any liability to any party for any loss, damage, or disruption caused by errors or omissions, whether such errors or omissions result from accident, negligence, or any other cause.

ISBN-13: 978-1-960727-14-5

Publisher: AAPPEAL, LLC Cranberry Township, PA www.eac-aappeal.com

INTRODUCTION

Welcome to the Black Empowerment Journal: A Reflective Guide for Leaders, Educators and Advocates. This transformative resource is designed to inspire and empower you in your pursuit of equity and inclusion within educational and professional spheres. Whether you are using this as a standalone guide or as a companion to Peter Carter's influential works, "A Black First: Leading Through Educational Barriers and Biases" and "The Blackness Continues: One Man's Ongoing Mission for Equitable Education," you are embarking on a journey of deep reflection and actionable change.

This journal invites you to explore the powerful themes of perseverance, leadership, and mission-driven impact that define Peter Carter's legacy. Through carefully crafted exercises and prompts, you will critically examine your role in dismantling biases, addressing systemic challenges, and creating truly inclusive spaces.

I find that writing things down and constantly reviewing my words helps them come to life. It is also easier to not have to remember an idea if it is on paper. I encourage you to do the same. There are no right or wrong responses, just let your mind flow and write down everything. Even if you stray from the original question, keep writing, those thoughts may be the answer to a future or lingering question. Quite often for me, weeks later an idea will resonate, and I know I had already written something down in my notebook. Carry this journal with you, and your ideas will come to life…

Enjoy!

How to Use This Journal

1. Approach each section as a call to action. Engage deeply with the reflective prompts and exercises, allowing yourself to explore uncomfortable truths and inspiring possibilities.

2. Set meaningful goals throughout your journey. Use the provided tools to create actionable plans for driving change in your sphere of influence.

3. Dive into the systemic challenges presented. Strive to understand the root causes of inequities and how they manifest in educational and professional settings.

4. Transform insights into impact. Each activity is designed to help you bridge the gap between reflection and action. Commit to implementing the strategies you develop.

5. Revisit and revise regularly. This is a living document meant to grow with you. Return to your reflections and goals, updating them as you gain new perspectives and experiences.

6. Connect with others. Consider forming or joining a study group to discuss your insights and plans, fostering a community dedicated to equitable change.

Remember, this journey is about personal growth, professional development, and societal transformation. Approach each section with an open mind, a willingness to challenge your assumptions, and a commitment to driving lasting change in education and beyond. Let us begin our exploration of leadership, advocacy, and the ongoing quest for equity and excellence, inspired by Peter Carter's unwavering dedication to creating equitable opportunities for all.

PART ONE

A BLACK FIRST
Leading Through Educational Barriers and Biases

The layout of the pages correspond to the sections in the book.

Chapter 1. The Beginning

Chapter 2. Uptown Manhattan

Chapter 3. Citizenship

Chapter 4. Brooklyn

Chapter 5. Regis High School and My Mother

Chapter 6. CYO Day Camp, Coney Island, Brooklyn

Chapter 7. The Bronx and Fordham University

Chapter 8. Job Hunting and My First Job

Chapter 9. The Funeral, the Wedding, and the Birth

Chapter 10. Moving in and Moving on, and Another Birth

Chapter 11. Another Journey Begins: Bedford-Stuyvesant and Wyandanch

Chapter 12. Meanwhile . . .

Chapter 13. Gauger Middle School: Newark, Delaware

Chapter 14. The New Jersey Ride Begins: Franklin Middle School, Metuchen

Chapter 15. Irvington, New Jersey: Its Board, Its Government, and Its Essence

Chapter 16. Roselle, New Jersey: My First Superintendency

Chapter 17. New Jersey Department of Education: Essex County Office

Chapter 18. A Mental Pause

Chapter 19. The Return to Irvington, New Jersey

Chapter 20. Just Before the End

Chapter 21. Ringwood, New Jersey: The Final Frontier

Chapter 1: The Beginning

Chapter Summary: Peter reflects on his early memories of arriving in America as a young child, emphasizing the cultural and societal differences he encountered. The narrative explores his early education, family dynamics, and the impact of living with his grandmother in Harlem. Through vivid storytelling, he describes how his mother and grandmother shaped his early years, including their struggles and resilience.

Objectives:

- Understand the impact of early childhood experiences on personal development.
- Explore the importance of family influence and cultural identity during formative years.
- Reflect on your earliest memory of learning and how it shaped your perception of education and success.

Reflection Questions

1. How have your early childhood experiences influenced your personal development?

2. In what ways has your family and cultural background shaped your identity?

3. What is your earliest memory of learning, and how did it impact your view of education?

Activities

1. Create a timeline of significant events from your childhood, highlighting moments that shaped your cultural identity.

2. Write a letter to your younger self, offering advice based on what you have learned about the importance of early experiences.

3. Interview an older family member about their early memories and compare them to your own.

Chapter 2: Uptown Manhattan

Chapter Summary: This chapter delves into Peter's first formal schooling experience at St. Catherine of Genoa Parochial School in Harlem. Despite financial hardships and racial and cultural differences, he excelled academically. The chapter also touches on social interactions, early lessons in gender differences, and the challenges of adapting to a new environment in an urban setting.

Objectives:

- Explore the significance of early education and its role in shaping long-term success.
- Analyze the impact of racial and cultural assimilation on self-identity.
- Understand the role of perseverance and ambition in overcoming childhood adversities.

Reflection Questions

1. How did your early education experiences shape your academic journey?

2. What challenges did you face in assimilating to a new cultural or educational environment??

3. How has perseverance played a role in overcoming obstacles in your life?

Activities

1. Write a personal essay about a time when you had to adapt to a new environment and the lessons you learned.

2. Create a vision board representing your educational and career aspirations, inspired by your early experiences.

3. Research and present on the educational experiences of first-generation immigrants in your community.

Chapter 3: Citizenship

Chapter Summary: In this chapter, Peter shares the story of his mother's journey toward becoming a naturalized citizen of the United States. He highlights the racial discrimination they faced during the naturalization process and the pride his mother took in becoming an American citizen. This chapter illustrates the emotional and symbolic significance of gaining citizenship in the face of systemic bias.

Objectives:

- Understand the emotional and practical challenges of immigrant life in the pursuit of citizenship.
- Reflect on the racial disparities faced during the naturalization process.
- Analyze how racial discrimination during childhood can shape one's worldview.

Reflection Questions

1. How has the concept of citizenship impacted your life or the lives of those close to you?

2. What are your thoughts on the challenges immigrants face in pursuing citizenship?

3. How can early experiences with discrimination shape a person's perspective on society?

Activities

1. Research the current naturalization process and create a flowchart illustrating the steps involved.

2. Write a fictional diary entry from the perspective of an immigrant pursuing citizenship.

3. Organize a class debate on the topic of immigration and citizenship policies.

Chapter 4: Brooklyn

Chapter Summary: This chapter recounts Peter's move from Manhattan to Brooklyn and the newfound freedom he felt in the housing project. It details his experiences with his new living environment, school life at St. Agnes Parochial School, and the diverse community around him. The chapter highlights his achievements as an altar server and his significant academic success, including receiving a full scholarship to Regis High School, a prestigious Jesuit school in Manhattan.

Objectives:

- Examine the impact of relocation on personal development and community integration.
- Explore the role of academic and extracurricular activities in shaping identity and success.
- Analyze the influence of socio-economic and ethnic diversity on childhood experiences.
- Reflect on the significance of personal achievements and community recognition in overcoming challenges.

Reflection Questions

1. How has moving to a new place impacted your personal growth and sense of community?

2. What role have extracurricular activities played in shaping your identity and success?

3. How has exposure to diverse socio-economic and ethnic backgrounds influenced your worldview?

Activities

1. Create a photo essay or collage representing the diversity in your community or school.

2. Write a reflection on a personal achievement and how it has influenced your life path.

3. Interview someone who has relocated to a new city or country about their experiences adapting to a new environment.

Chapter 5: Regis High School and My Mother

Chapter Summary: This chapter contrasts the influences of Regis High School and Peter's mother. In 1957, he and his mother meet the Regis Headmaster, revealing her unspoken approval of the school's challenging environment. Peter reflects on his early years with his mother, who, despite health and financial struggles, emphasized gender equality and high expectations. At Regis, known for its rigorous standards, Peter faced racial challenges and prejudice but also found support. The chapter concludes with a tense encounter with police detectives, highlighting the racial tensions of the era.

Objectives:

- Understand how parental influence shapes educational and personal resilience.
- Analyze the impact of racial dynamics in academic and social environments.
- Develop strategies for addressing personal and social challenges.

Reflection Questions

1. How has parental influence shaped your educational journey and personal resilience?

2. What challenges have you faced in academic or social environments due to your background?

3. What strategies have you developed to overcome personal and social challenges?

Activities

1. Write a letter of appreciation to someone who has positively influenced your educational journey.

2. Create a mind map illustrating the various influences on your personal and academic development.

3. Develop a personal action plan for addressing a current challenge in your life.

Chapter 6: CYO Day Camp, Coney Island, Brooklyn

Chapter Summary: The chapter details Peter's ten summers working at CYO Day Camp in Coney Island, Brooklyn, starting as a junior counselor and advancing to supervisory roles. The camp, part of the Catholic Youth Organization, became a transformative experience where he learned to navigate a predominantly white environment and develop essential administrative skills. Under the stern yet influential camp director, Mr. R, Peter gained insights into leadership and management. The camp fostered lasting friendships and provided a platform for personal growth, bridging racial and social gaps through shared experiences.

Objectives:

- Explore the impact of early work experiences on professional development.
- Understand the role of mentorship and leadership in personal growth.
- Examine the dynamics of racial integration in a predominantly white environment.

Reflection Questions

1. How have your early work experiences shaped your professional development?

2. Who has been a significant mentor in your life, and how have they influenced you?

3. What challenges have you faced in environments where you were part of a minority group?

Activities

1. Create a timeline of your work experiences, highlighting key skills learned and challenges overcome.

2. Write a thank-you letter to a mentor who has positively impacted your life.

3. Develop a presentation on strategies for promoting diversity and inclusion in work or school environments.

Chapter 7: The Bronx and Fordham University

Chapter Summary: The chapter recounts Peter's transition from Brooklyn to The Bronx to attend Fordham University, thanks to a scholarship arranged by his mother. At Fordham, Peter faced a predominantly white student body and navigated numerous challenges as one of the few Black students. He became a prominent campus politician, serving as Vice President and Treasurer of the Freshman Class, and played a key role in organizing concerts and events. Despite facing racial barriers, including a significant loss in the bid for student body president he gained valuable experiences in leadership and resilience. The chapter concludes with Peter's graduation in 1965 and the passing of his mother, reflecting on the highs and lows of his college years.

Objectives:

- Analyze the impact of attending a predominantly white institution on personal and professional development.
- Explore the dynamics of student politics and leadership in a diverse environment.
- Understand the emotional and social challenges associated with navigating racial barriers in academic settings.

Reflection Questions

1. How has your educational environment influenced your personal and professional growth?

2. What experiences have you had with student leadership or campus politics?

3. How have you navigated challenges related to diversity and inclusion in your academic or professional life?

Activities

1. Research and present on the history of diversity and inclusion initiatives at your school or a local university.

2. Organize a mock student government election, focusing on issues of diversity and representation a thank-you letter to a mentor who has positively impacted your life.

3. Write a personal essay about a time when you had to overcome a barrier or challenge in an academic or professional setting a presentation on strategies for promoting diversity and inclusion in work or school environments.

Chapter 8: Job Hunting and My First Job

Chapter Summary: The chapter recounts Peter's early work experiences, starting with an on-campus job at the university library, progressing to a part-time role in a major department store, and culminating in the pursuit of a teaching career. Peter reflects on the diverse job roles he undertook, from working as a library messenger to a department store clerk, and the experiences that shaped his professional journey. He highlights the importance of these early jobs in building his work ethic and resilience. His transition to teaching, particularly at Nazareth High School, was marked by both professional and personal growth. The chapter also touches on the challenges of navigating racial prejudices in job searches and the profound impact of early work experiences on his career.

Objectives:

- Understand the evolution of early job experiences and their influence on career development.
- Reflect on the impact of overcoming challenges and biases in the workplace.
- Recognize the significance of work ethic and resilience in achieving professional goals.

Reflection Questions

1. How has your early job experiences influenced your career path?

2. What challenges have you faced in the workplace, and how did you overcome them?

3. How has your work ethic evolved through your various job experiences?

Activities

1. Create a skills inventory based on your work experiences and identify areas for growth.

2. Write a reflection on a challenging work situation and the lessons learned from it.

3. Develop a career roadmap, outlining your professional goals and the steps needed to achieve them.

Chapter 9: The Funeral, the Wedding, and the Birth

Chapter Summary: The chapter explores significant life events that occurred during Peter's transition from college to adulthood. It begins with his experiences dating two women from Thomas More College, reflecting on the role of his mother and the impact of parental approval on his relationships. The chapter then shifts to the emotional period of his mother's illness and funeral, highlighting the diverse group of attendees and the financial challenges associated with the event. The narrative continues with his marriage to Laura, a woman from Brooklyn, and their unique wedding ceremony, which included an eclectic mix of bridal and groomsmen. The chapter concludes with the birth of their daughter, detailing the logistical challenges and personal growth experienced during this significant life event.

Objectives:

- Reflect on the impact of significant life events, including relationships, family milestones, and personal growth.
- Understand the challenges and emotional experiences associated with major life transitions such as marriage and parenthood.
- Explore the influence of family dynamics and societal expectations on personal decisions and relationships.

Reflection Questions

1. How have significant life events shaped your personal growth and worldview?

2. What challenges have you faced during major life transitions?

3. How have family dynamics and societal expectations influenced your personal decisions?

Activities

1. Create a personal timeline highlighting significant life events and their impact on your growth.

2. Write a reflective essay on a major life transition you have experienced, and the lessons learned.

3. Interview family members about their experiences with significant life events and compare them to your own.

Chapter 10: Moving in and Moving on, and Another Birth

Chapter Summary: The chapter details Peter's struggle with racial discrimination while searching for a new apartment for his growing family. After legal action, he secured a place in East Flatbush as the first Black family in the building. The chapter also highlights his fulfilling teaching experiences at Nazareth and Brooklyn Prep, his successful transition to a corporate sales role, and the ease of his second child's birth compared to earlier challenges. The chapter concludes with his return to education through a new role aimed at improving inner-city youth academic performance.

Objectives:

- Explore the challenges and successes encountered in finding suitable housing amid racial discrimination.
- Reflect on the professional growth and impact of teaching at different educational institutions.
- Examine the transition from teaching to a corporate career and the subsequent return to education.

Reflection Questions

1. Have you or someone you know experienced discrimination in housing or other areas of life?

2. How have your professional experiences in different fields contributed to your growth?

3. What factors would you consider when making a career transition?

Activities

1. Research fair housing laws and create an informational brochure on tenant rights.

2. Write a comparative essay on the pros and cons of working in education versus the corporate world.

3. Develop a personal mission statement that reflects your professional values and goals.

Chapter 11: Another Journey Begins: Bedford-Stuyvesant and Wyandanch

Chapter Summary: The chapter describes Peter's transition from a role at an inner-city school in Brooklyn to becoming the Director of Elementary and Secondary Education in Wyandanch, Long Island. At the New Catholic High School, he managed a diverse team and navigated racial and logistical challenges while improving student outcomes. In Wyandanch, he faced resistance from some school staff and board members but worked to enhance educational stability. During this time, Peter completed a master's in educational administration, relocated to Uniondale, Long Island, where his family thrived, and later moved to Delaware for his first principalship. The chapter highlights his commitment to education and overcoming racial barriers in different settings.

Objectives:

- Examine the challenges and strategies for managing diverse teams in urban educational settings.
- Analyze the impact of resistance to change in school districts and methods for promoting educational stability.
- Understand the complexities of transitioning between different educational roles and environments.

Reflection Questions

1. What challenges do educational leaders face when implementing change in diverse communities?

2. How can one effectively overcome resistance when in a leadership position?

3. How have your various roles contributed to your personal and professional growth?

Activities:

1. Create a case study on a local school facing challenges and propose solutions.

2. Develop a leadership strategy for promoting diversity and inclusion in an educational setting.

3. Write a reflection on a time when you faced resistance while trying to implement a change or new idea.

Chapter 12: Meanwhile . . .

Chapter Summary: The chapter provides a series of personal anecdotes and reflections, beginning with Peter's experiences related to his grandmother's death and her quirks, including her devotion to St. Jude and the management of her estate. Peter recounts inheriting and then selling his grandmother's brownstone, which he later regretted. The chapter also touches on his academic journey at Hofstra University, including his near completion of a doctoral degree and a significant relationship with a woman who would later assist his daughter in obtaining her doctoral degree. The chapter serves as a collection of personal reflections and lessons learned from these experiences.

Objectives:

- Reflect on the personal challenges and life lessons learned from managing family responsibilities and property.
- Understand the impact of academic pursuits and relationships on personal and professional development.
- Recognize how personal experiences and relationships can shape one's career and life choices.

Reflection Questions

1. How have personal responsibilities influenced your academic or professional pursuits?

2. What life lessons have you learned from managing personal or family matters?

3. How have your relationships shaped your career and life choices?

Activities:

1. Create a personal balance sheet of life experiences, listing challenges faced and lessons learned.

2. Write a reflective essay on how a significant relationship has influenced your personal or professional development.

3. Develop a five-year plan that integrates your personal, academic, and professional goals.

Chapter 13: Gauger Middle School: Newark, Delaware

Chapter Summary: The chapter reflects Peter's time as the principal of Gauger Middle School in Newark, Delaware. He discusses the challenges of leading a diverse school community amid racial tensions and desegregation. He also navigated a unique school design with "wall-less" classrooms and managed the integration of students from different socioeconomic and racial backgrounds, including two hundred Black students from Wilmington. Despite facing a teacher strike and managing a divided staff, he successfully raised student achievement and improved staff morale. The chapter also highlights his personal life, including his second marriage and the eventual amicable divorce. The chapter ends with reflections on leadership, missed promotions, and recognizing talent.

Objectives:

- Understand the complexities of leading a school through racial desegregation and staff challenges.
- Reflect on the role of leadership in overcoming systemic and societal barriers in education.
- Identify the importance of perseverance, adaptability, and relationship-building in challenging work environments.

Reflection Questions

1. How can educational leaders effectively address racial tensions and promote inclusivity?

2. What strategies can be employed to improve student achievement in challenging environments?

3. How does perseverance and adaptability contribute to success in difficult work situations?

Activities:

1. Research a historical case of school desegregation and create a presentation on its challenges and outcomes.

2. Develop a hypothetical action plan for improving student achievement in a diverse, underperforming school.

3. Write a reflection on a time when you had to adapt to a challenging situation and the lessons you learned.

Chapter 14: The New Jersey Ride Begins: Franklin Middle School, Metuchen

Chapter Summary: The chapter reflects on Peter's journey as the first Black principal in a predominantly white suburban district in New Jersey. Facing subtle racism and resistance, he transformed Franklin Middle School from a rigid institution to a more student-centered environment. His creative problem-solving and leadership improved student performance despite opposition from staff and students. The chapter also highlights the political dynamics of education, revealing how success often requires navigating local politics and balancing educational goals with political realities. This experience laid the foundation for his later roles in central office administration and beyond.

Objectives:

- Understand the personal and professional challenges faced as a Black principal in a predominantly white suburban district.
- Explore the importance of leadership and creative problem-solving in transforming a school culture.
- Learn about the balance and navigation of educational administration and community politics in shaping school environments.

Reflection Questions

1. How can leaders effectively navigate and address racial biases in professional settings?

2. What strategies can be employed to transform a resistant school culture?

3. How does community politics influence educational administration and decision-making?

Activities:

1. Create a diversity and inclusion initiative for a hypothetical school facing similar challenges.

2. Role-play a scenario where you must address resistance to change in a school setting.

3. Research and present on successful school transformation case studies.

Chapter 15: Irvington, New Jersey: Its Board, Its Government, and Its Essence

Chapter Summary: In 1986, Peter becomes Assistant Superintendent in Irvington, New Jersey, where racial and political tensions run high. Surrounded by resistant colleagues, he faces an uphill battle in improving the district's failing schools, particularly Irvington High School. Despite the low expectations and a challenging environment, he leads a dramatic improvement in student performance on the statewide High School Proficiency Test. His leadership earns him respect and admiration, even from initial critics, culminating in an offer for a superintendent position in Roselle, New Jersey.

Objectives:

- Understand the impact of race and politics on educational leadership.
- Analyze strategies for improving student performance in underperforming schools.
- Explore how resilience and leadership can shift perceptions and overcome biases.

Reflection Questions

1. How do racial and political dynamics affect educational leadership and decision-making?

2. What strategies can be implemented to improve student performance in challenging environments?

3. How can leaders demonstrate resilience in the face of adversity and bias?

Activities:

1. Develop a strategic plan to improve student performance in a hypothetical underperforming school.

2. Write a case study analysis of a school district that successfully navigated racial and political tensions.

3. Create a personal resilience toolkit with strategies for overcoming professional challenges.

Chapter 16: Roselle, New Jersey: My First Superintendency

Chapter Summary: In Roselle, New Jersey, Peter experiences his first superintendency, facing significant racial and political challenges. The presence of White supremacist board members and unsupportive African American colleagues made his leadership difficult. Despite these obstacles, he hired an exceptional secretary and collaborated with the Union County Superintendent to achieve meaningful improvements, including securing long-overdue textbooks for students. The district was plagued by weak leadership, political factions, and lack of support. Although his tenure in Roselle was brief and challenging, the guidance of a trusted mentor and former colleague provided encouragement and led to his next significant role as Essex County Superintendent of Schools in 1989.

Objectives:

- Understand the complexities of leadership in a racially and politically charged environment.
- Analyze how resilience and strategic relationships can support progress despite adversity.
- Identify the key challenges and successes in educational leadership during difficult circumstances.

Reflection Questions

1. How can educational leaders navigate complex racial and political dynamics?

2. What role do strategic relationships play in achieving progress in challenging environments?

3. How can one measure success in educational leadership when facing significant obstacles?

Activities:

1. Create a stakeholder map for a hypothetical school district, identifying key relationships and potential challenges.

2. Develop a crisis management plan for addressing racial or political conflicts in an educational setting.

3. Write a reflection on a personal or professional situation where you had to demonstrate resilience in the face of adversity.

Chapter 17: New Jersey Department of Education: Essex County Office

Chapter Summary: In his role as Essex County Superintendent of Schools, Peter navigates a complex environment initially met with skepticism from some colleagues and local officials. Despite facing obstacles such as a discriminatory police encounter and the political complexities of overseeing diverse districts, he successfully improves educational standards and manages significant issues, including the Newark school district's state takeover. His tenure includes administrative successes and challenges, such as addressing credential irregularities and managing controversial issues. Peter's effective leadership, grounded in his past experiences and strategic alliances, ultimately makes a significant impact on the county's educational landscape.

Objectives:

- Understand the dynamics of leading a diverse and politically complex educational environment.
- Examine the strategies used to overcome racial biases and political obstacles in a high-profile leadership role.
- Evaluate the impact of decisions on educational improvements and organizational management.

Reflection Questions

1. How can leaders effectively navigate racial and political challenges in educational administration?

2. What strategies can be employed to establish credibility in a new leadership role?

3. How do past experiences influence decision-making in complex educational environments?

Activities:

1. Create a case study analysis of a school district takeover, examining the challenges and potential solutions.

2. Develop a strategic plan for addressing credential irregularities in an educational system.

3. Role-play a scenario where you must navigate political complexities while implementing educational reforms.

Chapter 18: A Mental Pause

Chapter Summary: This chapter reflects on Peter's personal experiences with racism and prejudice in various settings. The narrative begins with an incident where he, a Black man, is stopped by a state trooper with no justifiable cause, but his "Driving While Black" cards help defuse the situation. It continues with stories of discrimination in retail and public spaces, where Peter faces scrutiny, unwarranted suspicion, and invisibility. Despite these challenges, he emphasizes his success through education and hard work, overcoming both personal and systemic barriers. The chapter concludes with Peter's return to a stressful role as Superintendent, motivated by a desire to make a difference for children.

Objectives:

- Recognize the impact of racial bias and discrimination in everyday experiences.
- Understanding coping mechanisms and strategies to address and overcome racial prejudice.
- Reflect on the resilience required to persist and succeed despite systemic and personal challenges.

Reflection Questions

1. How do every day experiences of discrimination impact personal and professional life?

2. What strategies can be employed to address and overcome racial prejudice?

3. How does resilience contribute to success in the face of systemic challenges?

Activities:

1. Write a reflective essay on a personal experience with discrimination or bias.

2. Create a resource guide for addressing and reporting incidents of racial discrimination.

3. Develop a personal resilience plan for overcoming systemic challenges in your field.

Chapter 19: The Return to Irvington, New Jersey

Chapter Summary: Returning to Irvington as Superintendent was a challenging yet crucial moment in Peter's career. Despite his initial success as a curriculum innovator, he faced a district in severe financial disarray, with an $8 million deficit. His first steps involved promoting capable staff, addressing budgetary issues, and tackling inefficiencies head-on. Despite facing resistance, including from the teachers' union and internal staff, Peter worked to stabilize the financial situation, ultimately turning the deficit into a $3 million surplus by the end of his tenure. His leadership also focused on improving educational outcomes, upgrading facilities, and addressing community issues.

Objectives:

- Analyze strategies to address severe financial deficits in an educational setting.
- Examine the impact of leadership decisions on organizational morale and effectiveness.
- Explore the role of community engagement and transparency in overcoming administrative challenges.

Reflection Questions

1. How can leaders effectively address financial crises in educational institutions?

2. What strategies can improve organizational morale during periods of significant change?

3. How does community engagement contribute to overcoming administrative challenges?

Activities:

1. Develop a financial recovery plan for a hypothetical school district facing a significant deficit.

2. Create a communication strategy for engaging stakeholders during a period of organizational change.

3. Design a community outreach program to improve transparency and trust in school administration.

Chapter 20: Just Before the End

Chapter Summary: In this penultimate chapter, Peter reflects on key individuals who inspired and supported the creation of his memoir. His daughter, Dr. Elizabeth Carter, receives the highest praise for her persistence in encouraging him to document his wealth of experiences he had to share. He also thanks Reverend Joseph M. McShane, the President of Fordham University, for his push to write about his many groundbreaking achievements as a Black man. Additionally, Peter expresses gratitude to the women who played vital roles in his life. He explains his literary choices, particularly the use of initials and first names, and the contrast of ethnic backgrounds in his narrative. Finally, he dedicates the book to his late mother, Bernice Mildred Camilla Carter.

Objectives:

- Recognize the importance of acknowledging support and influence of others in personal and professional achievements.
- Understand the significance of literary choices in shaping a narrative.
- Reflect on the role of family, mentors, and loved ones in shaping identity and career paths.

Reflection Questions

1. Who has played a significant role in shaping your personal and professional journey?

2. How do literary choices impact the way a story is told and received?

3. What role have mentors played in your life, and how have they influenced your path?

Activities:

1. Write a letter of appreciation to someone who has significantly influenced your life or career.

2. Create a mind map illustrating the key influences and relationships that have shaped your journey.

3. Develop a personal mission statement that reflects the values and lessons learned from mentors and loved ones.

Chapter 21: Ringwood, New Jersey: The Final Frontier

Chapter Summary: In this final chapter, Peter recounts his tenure as Superintendent in Ringwood, New Jersey, from 1999 to 2004. Despite the colder climate, the people of Ringwood were warm and welcoming. Peter implemented significant improvements, including new textbooks, security systems, and the state's first public middle school program for autistic children. His leadership was tested during 9/11, as he managed the district's response and ensured the safety of the students. Despite resistance from a few upon his arrival, Peter's commitment to communication and community engagement fostered a positive environment. Ultimately, he chose to retire in 2004, reflecting on his rewarding career. His retirement was celebrated by students, staff, and the community, honoring his lasting impact.

Objectives:

- Understand the complexities of leading a suburban school district and managing community relations.
- Learn the importance of proactive decision-making during crises and fostering communication.
- Reflect on the impact of leadership on education, particularly in creating inclusive programs.

Reflection Questions

1. How can educational leaders effectively manage community relations in diverse settings?

2. What strategies are crucial for decision-making during unexpected crises in educational settings?

3. How can leaders foster innovation and inclusivity in educational programs?

Activities:

1. Develop a crisis management plan for a school district facing an emergency.

2. Create a proposal for an innovative educational program that addresses a specific community need.

3. Write a reflection on your educational journey and how it might inform your future leadership approach.

PART TWO

THE BLACKNESS CONTINUES...
One Man's Ongoing Mission for Equitable Education

The layout of the pages correspond to the sections in the book.

Chapter 1. The Second Beginning

Chapter 2. Delaware - The Location of This Beginning

Chapter 3. Six Months in Plainfield, New Jersey

Chapter 4. R & R in Rehoboth Beach, Delaware

Chapter 5. Finding Something to Do

Chapter 6. Last Stop on the Interim Train: HOBOKEN.

Chapter 7. Inside the Hoboken Educational Experience

Chapter 8. Getting Out of Hoboken – Not Easy Either

Chapter 9. Lawyers, Courts, and More Lawyers

Chapter 10. District v District v State Department of Education

Chapter 11. Recess from the Courts / Mentoring of a Woman

Chapter 12. Back in Court – Almost – Then, Actually

Chapter 13. The Continuation Ends, Perhaps with a Bang AND a Whimper

Chapter 1: The Second Beginning

Chapter Summary: After retiring, Peter Carter's post-career journey began with a symbolic return to St. Patrick's Cathedral, honoring his mother's tradition and expressing gratitude for his career. Peter found himself in education again, this time teaching college courses on the foundations of American education. His classes often stirred discussions about the racial biases inherent in the education system. Peter's unique approach highlighted how education, like many institutions, was designed to serve a select group. His adjunct teaching at multiple universities revealed both the challenges of systemic racism and the personal fulfillment of making a difference in students' lives, despite facing continued prejudice in academic circles. Through teaching, Peter reflected on race, education, and the transformative power of addressing societal biases head-on.

Objectives:

- Examine the intersection of race and education in the American educational system.
- Analyze how historical biases have shaped and continue to influence modern educational institutions.
- Explore the impact of personal and societal biases on educational and professional environments.

Reflection Questions

1. How have your experiences shaped your understanding of racial biases in education?

2. What role can educators play in addressing systemic racism in schools?

3. How can personal reflection on biases lead to positive changes in educational settings?

Activities:

1. Create a timeline of significant events in American education, highlighting moments of progress and setbacks in addressing racial inequalities.

2. Write a reflective essay on a personal experience that revealed hidden biases in an educational or professional setting.

3. Develop a lesson plan that addresses a historical bias in education and proposes strategies for a more inclusive approach.

Chapter 2: Delaware – The Location of This Beginning

Chapter Summary: Peter recounts his decision to relocate from New Jersey to Delaware after retiring, drawn by its tax benefits and proximity to friends. He reflects on key moments, such as purchasing a new home, navigating car ownership, and building relationships with locals in his new community. Despite being one of the few African Americans in certain areas, Peter found camaraderie among diverse groups at the beach, restaurants, and a bookstore. These relationships helped him feel more at home. He also shares his brief return to the workforce as an Interim Superintendent, overcoming racial barriers to lead a New Jersey school district successfully.

Objectives:

- Examine the factors that influence post-retirement relocation decisions.
- Analyze the challenges and opportunities of integrating into a new community with a different demographic makeup.
- Explore strategies for maintaining professional identity and expertise during major life transitions.

Reflection Questions

1. What factors would you consider when relocating to a new community after retirement?

2. How can one maintain a personal identity while adapting to a new environment?

3. What strategies can be employed to overcome racial barriers in professional settings?

Activities:

1. Create a pros and cons list for relocating to a new community in retirement.

2. Role-play a scenario where you are integrating into a community with a different demographic makeup than your own.

3. Develop a personal action plan for maintaining professional skills and connections post-retirement.

Chapter 3: Six Months in Plainfield, New Jersey

Chapter Summary: In this chapter, Peter reflects on his brief but eventful tenure as an Interim Superintendent of Plainfield's school district. He brought two trusted professionals with him to tackle the challenges in an urban school district divided by socioeconomic lines. Despite political interference and skepticism from the school board, Peter maintained a student-first approach, implementing policies such as free breakfast and a test-based student handbook. His leadership team, known as "The Dream Team," worked tirelessly to improve the district. However, internal politics, lack of support from the Board of Education, and disregard for excellence led to the team's collective resignation after only six months. Peter emphasizes the potential for educational greatness in Plainfield, lamenting that the opportunity was lost due to personal and political agendas.

Objectives:

- Examine the challenges of implementing reform in urban school districts with diverse socioeconomic backgrounds.
- Analyze the impact of political dynamics on educational leadership and district performance.
- Explore strategies for maintaining a student-centered approach in the face of administrative and political obstacles.

Reflection Questions

1. How can educational leaders maintain a student-first approach amid political pressures?

2. What strategies can be employed to build support for reform efforts in challenging environments?

3. How does short-term leadership impact long-term educational outcomes?

Activities:

1. Create a mock strategic plan for a school district facing similar challenges to Plainfield.

2. Write a case study analysis of a successful school district turnaround, identifying key factors for success.

3. Develop a communication strategy for building stakeholder support in a politically charged educational environment.

Chapter 4: R & R in Rehoboth Beach, Delaware

Chapter Summary: In January 2008, after a series of medical procedures, Peter reflects on life, career, and health while enjoying the calm of Rehoboth Beach, Delaware. This period of rest and recuperation allows for introspection, drawing parallels between the discipline of sports and the challenges of education, a profession often undervalued. He finds solace in his walks along the boardwalk and uses the time to consider the complexities of education as a political landscape, often led by officials with little practical understanding. In a unique contrast, he is embraced in a leadership role by his mostly white neighbors in his condominium community, a refreshing experience after feeling unacknowledged in the academic setting. This chapter explores themes of resilience, self-reflection, and the ongoing struggle for respect and fulfillment in both personal and professional arenas.

Objectives:

- Reflect on health challenges' impact on life direction and personal fulfillment.
- Understand education's political dynamics and effects on educators and students.
- Examine the significance of mutual respect in diverse social and professional contexts.

Reflection Questions

1. How can periods of rest and reflection contribute to professional growth and personal insight?

2. What parallels can you draw between your field of expertise and other disciplines?

3. How does community acceptance impact personal well-being and professional outlook?

Activities:

1. Create a personal wellness plan that integrates professional goals and health considerations.

2. Write a reflective essay on a time when you felt truly accepted in a new environment and its impact.

3. Develop a list of strategies for maintaining perspective and balance in a politically charged work environment.

Chapter 5: Finding Something to Do

Chapter Summary: In winter and spring of 2008, quiet days and daily walks on Rehoboth's Boardwalk provided both health benefits and a unique vantage into southern Delaware's community dynamics. With few winter activities, Peter spent time on the local Homeowners Association, observing regional development practices and promoting property retention among Black homeowners. Peter noted the deep historical connections within communities of Black and White families, shaped by shared heritage and socioeconomic ties. Observing the labor contributions of Central American immigrants in agriculture and landscaping, Peter drew parallels to past racial labor divides. As summer approached, the relative solitude of this reflection period ended with a call back to educational leadership in New Jersey.

Objectives:

- Understand socio-economic and racial dynamics in rural Delaware communities.
- Recognize challenges and opportunities for minority homeowners in retaining ancestral properties.
- Explore immigrant laborers' contributions and challenges in agricultural and landscaping industries.

Reflection Questions

1. How do historical community ties impact current social and economic dynamics?

2. What strategies can support minority homeowners in retaining and passing down property?

3. How do immigrant labor patterns reflect or differ from historical racial labor divides?

Activities:

1. Research and present on the history of property ownership and transfer in a specific minority community.

2. Create a resource guide for minority homeowners on property retention and generational wealth building.

3. Develop a comparative analysis of historical and current labor patterns in a specific industry or region.

Chapter 6: Last Stop on the Interim Train: HOBOKEN

Chapter Summary: The chapter details Peter reflection on his interim role in Hoboken's school district, navigating a web of challenges and corruption within the city's Board of Education. Hoboken, a bustling hub with a young professional population, held contrasting worlds of wealth and neglect. Peter encountered entrenched corrupt practices, including misuse of district resources like school buses and questionable financial arrangements with local businesses. Despite the backlash, he took decisive steps to uphold integrity, including terminating those involved in fraudulent activities. With a focus on restoring order, Peter's leadership eventually transitioned from damage control to supporting education, exemplified by assembling a skilled administrative team to foster improvement in teaching and learning.

Objectives:

- Understand the impact of entrenched corruption on public institutions and the education system.
- Recognize the importance of ethical leadership in addressing and preventing misconduct.
- Explore effective strategies for reforming administrative practices to support educational integrity.

Reflection Questions

1. How can leaders effectively address corruption in educational institutions?

2. What challenges might arise when implementing ethical reforms in a system with entrenched misconduct?

3. How does corruption in education impact students and the broader community?

Activities:

1. Develop an ethical leadership plan for a hypothetical school district facing corruption issues.

2. Create a case study analysis of a successful educational reform that addressed systemic integrity problems.

3. Design a workshop for school administrators on identifying and preventing corrupt practices in education.

Chapter 7: Inside the Hoboken Educational Experience

Chapter Summary: In this chapter, Peter explores his experiences within the Hoboken school district, highlighting the complex dynamics between academics and athletics, school culture, and leadership challenges. He details the district's commitment to sports, the talents of the drama program, and interactions with the local community. Peter also reflects on educational inequities, staff issues, and unique student incidents that necessitated disciplinary action. Addressing facilities and infrastructure, he discusses the flooding in certain schools and strategic changes to student placements to alleviate overcrowding. Throughout, Peter remains focused on enhancing student experiences and safety, despite numerous obstacles, to foster a positive educational environment.

Objectives:

- Analyze the balance between academic priorities and extracurricular activities in urban school districts.
- Examine the impact of leadership decisions on student experiences and educational equity in diverse educational settings.
- Explore strategies for improving school safety, resource allocation, and inclusivity in the face of infrastructure and overcrowding challenges.

Reflection Questions

1. How can school leaders balance academic priorities with extracurricular activities like sports and drama?

2. What strategies can be employed to address educational inequities within a diverse school district?

3. How might infrastructure challenges impact the overall learning environment and student safety?

Activities:

1. Create a strategic plan to address overcrowding and infrastructure issues in a school district.

2. Develop a proposal for enhancing inclusivity and equity in school programs and resources.

3. Design a community engagement initiative to improve school-community relationships.

Chapter 8: Getting Out of Hoboken – Not Easy Either

Chapter Summary: The chapter recounts Peter's experiences while serving as an interim superintendent in Hoboken. Although his contract was initially for one year, the school board extended it, appreciating the positive direction he had brought to the district. He describes the difficulties of managing Hoboken's school system under a restrictive salary cap imposed by a less-than-supportive governor, whose policies made it challenging to attract qualified candidates for leadership roles. Peter navigated political obstacles, community dynamics, and personal adjustments as he commuted from Delaware and enjoyed weekends in New York City. After months of back-and-forth negotiations, Peter finally secured a permanent superintendent's appointment for Hoboken, marking the end of his interim tenure. Reflecting on this time, Peter describes a bittersweet farewell to public education, closing a chapter of dedicated service and resilience.

Objectives:

- Understand the challenges of interim leadership and navigating political limitations in public education.
- Explore the balance between professional obligations and personal adaptation in a temporary role.
- Recognize the impact of external political influences on educational leadership and community relations..

Reflection Questions

1. How can educational leaders effectively navigate political constraints while maintaining focus on student needs?

2. What strategies can be employed to ensure continuity of positive changes during leadership transitions?

3. How might personal sacrifices in a temporary leadership role impact long-term career decisions?

Activities:

1. Create a transition plan for handing over leadership responsibilities in an interim role.

2. Develop a strategy for maintaining work-life balance while commuting long distances for a temporary position.

3. Write a reflection on the challenges and rewards of serving in an interim leadership capacity.

Chapter 9: Lawyers, Courts, and More Lawyers

Chapter Summary: Peter delves into his extensive experiences navigating the legal system, primarily in cases involving school districts and institutional child abuse. He reflects on the complex world of law, where lawyers operate with objective flexibility, arguing both sides as needed. Peter's role, driven by financial incentive, involved presenting objective data and analysis to defend school districts against allegations of negligence. Through case studies, he illustrates his impartial approach and commitment to the "WIN"—demonstrating how race and personal beliefs became secondary to his role as a hired expert. His professional detachment allowed him to contribute to favorable outcomes for his clients while maintaining a clear boundary from the emotional complexities of each case.

Objectives:

- Analyze the role of expert witnesses in legal cases involving educational institutions and child safety.
- Examine the ethical considerations and professional detachment required when defending against allegations of institutional negligence.
- Explore the balance between objectivity and personal values in high-stakes legal proceedings related to education.

Reflection Questions

1. How can professionals maintain objectivity when personal beliefs conflict with their professional role?

2. What ethical considerations arise when defending institutions against allegations of negligence?

3. How might expertise in education contribute to effective legal representation in school-related cases?

Activities:

1. Conduct a mock trial scenario involving a school district negligence case.

2. Develop a code of ethics for educational consultants working in legal settings.

3. Create a presentation on the intersection of education, law, and ethics in institutional child abuse cases.

Chapter 10: District v District v State Department of Education

Chapter Summary: In this chapter, Peter unpacks the complex dynamics of New Jersey's school district configurations, where municipalities employ various K-12, K-8, and 7-12 setups. He shares his experiences as an educational expert witness, advocating for districts seeking to change their send-receive partnerships. Highlighting his role in conducting Feasibility Studies, Peter discusses the intricacies of evaluating academic, demographic, and financial factors while ensuring racial neutrality. Through two cases, he shows how his thorough research and persuasion shaped successful outcomes for his clients, revealing the challenges and rewards of navigating the educational, political, and social landscapes of school district relationships in New Jersey.

Objectives:

- Understand the structure and variations in a school district configurations.
- Learn about the role of a Feasibility Study in educational send-receive relationships.
- Recognize the legal and social complexities involved in educational expert witness cases.

Reflection Questions

1. How do different school district configurations impact educational equity and resource allocation?

2. What factors should be considered when evaluating the feasibility of changing district partnerships?

3. How can expert witnesses balance objectivity with advocacy in educational legal cases?

Activities:

1. Conduct a mock Feasibility Study for a hypothetical school district seeking to change its send-receive relationship.

2. Create a comparative analysis of different K-12 district configurations and their impacts on student outcomes.

3. Develop a presentation on the role of expert witnesses in shaping educational policy through legal channels.

Chapter 11: Recess from the Courts / Mentoring of a Woman

Chapter Summary: In this chapter, Peter reflects on his mentorship of an exceptional educator, MVG, who began as a cooperating teacher and eventually achieved her goal of becoming a superintendent. His role was instrumental in her professional ascent, but her talent, commitment, and empathy for her students were equally impactful. Throughout her journey, Peter highlighted the importance of professionalism, mutual respect, and the ways mentorship transcends racial and cultural divides. This story underscores that success is not defined by race but by shared human values and dedication. In mentoring MVG, Peter emphasized that leading with respect and support can shape not only careers but also communities, regardless of background.

Objectives:

- Recognize the impact of supportive mentorship on professional growth and leadership development.
- Explore how mutual respect and understanding can overcome social and racial barriers in professional relationships.
- Understand the value of aligning professional conduct with personal values to foster meaningful educational environments.

Reflection Questions

1. How can mentorship contribute to breaking barriers in educational leadership?

2. What qualities make an effective mentor in the field of education?

3. How can professionals from diverse backgrounds build strong, supportive relationships?

Activities:

1. Design a cross-cultural mentorship initiative that addresses specific challenges in educational leadership.

2. Analyze a case study of a successful mentorship relationship that overcame significant cultural or social barriers.

3. Develop a workshop outline for building inclusive professional networks in diverse educational settings.

Chapter 12: Back in Court – Almost – Then, Actually

Chapter Summary: In Chapter 12, Peter recounts three separate cases involving New Jersey school districts with distinct educational and racial issues. Two of the cases—attempted consolidations or changes to school sending arrangements—never reached court, one due to financial constraints and another influenced by politics. The third case, however, did proceed to court. Here, he skillfully advocated for a school district's right to shift its sending relationship, arguing that the proposed change would benefit students. Despite facing age-based and racial biases from opposing counsel, Peter's expertise and professionalism led to a favorable outcome for his client. His story demonstrates that resilience and excellence can overcome discrimination and that justice, while complex, ultimately serves the students..

Objectives:

- Understand the complexities and obstacles in school district legal disputes, including financial, political, and social factors.
- Recognize the role of resilience and professionalism in navigating bias and personal attacks in the courtroom.
- Explore the importance of advocating student welfare amid administrative and legal challenges.

Reflection Questions

1. How can educational leaders effectively navigate legal challenges while prioritizing student needs?

2. What strategies can be employed to maintain professionalism in the face of personal attacks or bias?

3. How do financial and political factors influence educational legal disputes?

Activities:

1. Conduct a role-play scenario of a courtroom debate on a school district sending relationship change.

2. Develop a strategy for addressing age-based and racial biases in professional settings.

3. Create a decision-making framework for evaluating the merits of pursuing legal action in educational disputes.

Chapter 13: The Continuation Ends, Perhaps with a Bang AND a Whimper

Chapter Summary: In Chapter 13, Peter reflects on his legal journey and the closing chapter of his career, culminating in a final case to improve educational opportunities for a school district. Despite initial opposition, his reputation and expertise led the opposing district to withdraw. Peter broadens his reflections to examine the African American experience in America, questioning why disparities persist despite efforts toward progress. He stresses the need for role models and encouragement within Black communities, emphasizing resilience over self-pity. Peter concludes with a hopeful message, urging continued pursuit of success for Black Americans and more "firsts" turned into lasting legacies.

Objectives:

- Understand the impact of perseverance and reputation in resolving complex legal issues.
- Reflect on the systemic and personal challenges faced by African Americans striving for success.
- Explore strategies to support and inspire the next generation of African American leaders.

Reflection Questions

1. How can individuals leverage their reputation and expertise to effect positive change in their field?

2. What ongoing challenges do African Americans face in pursuing educational and professional success?

3. How can we create more opportunities for "firsts" to become lasting legacies in various fields?

Activities:

1. Create a strategic plan for a community-based program that supports emerging leaders from underrepresented groups.

2. Draft a proposal for an institutional policy that promotes equity and representation in leadership positions.

3. Design a public awareness campaign to highlight and celebrate diverse "firsts" in various professional fields.

Final Words

Congratulations on completing the reflection questions and exercises in this workbook. Throughout these chapters, you have explored themes of perseverance, leadership, inclusivity, and resilience. You have confronted challenges, celebrated victories, and gained insights into what it means to lead with integrity, courage, and compassion. Now, as you move forward, remember that this journey is ongoing. The real work begins when you apply these lessons to your daily life—whether in your career, community, or personal relationships.

Just as Peter E. Carter navigated barriers and biases to become a trailblazer in education and leadership, you, too, can leave a lasting impact. Your unique story, talents, and contributions matter. Keep elevating your value, and do not stop pushing boundaries. Always seek opportunities to learn, grow, and make a difference for yourself and others.

Additional Reflection and Notes

Additional Reflection and Notes

Additional Reflection and Notes

Additional Reflection and Notes

About the Authors

Dr. Elizabeth A. Carter is an insurance professional, performance improvement leader, speaker, and author. With over 25 years working in corporate settings in a financial discipline, Dr. Carter has a unique passion for financial acumen and knowledge empowerment that has provided her the opportunity to lead, mentor, and develop others in the areas of strategy and financial analysis, performance improvement, and talent development for profit and nonprofit organizations.

She is the CEO of AAPPEAL, LLC, a company branded on her four passions of leadership, engagement, analytics, and performance. She offers training programs, facilitated sessions, keynote presentations, and one-on-one coaching to help individuals and companies close the gaps between their current situations and desired aspirations. Visit her website at www.eac-aappeal.com.

Dr. Carter holds a PhD in education specializing in training and performance improvement from Capella University. She holds an MS in education in the same specialization from Capella University and an MBA in management from the New York Institute of Technology. She earned a BBA in marketing from Hofstra University. Further, she holds the Chartered Property Casualty Underwriter designation and is a Distinguished Toastmaster.

A graduate of Fordham University with a Bachelor's degree in Classical Languages, and Hofstra University with Master's degree in Educational Administration, **Peter E. Carter** labored in the vineyards of both private and public school education from 1965 when he began as a Teacher of Latin and English at Nazareth Regional High School in Brooklyn, New York, until his retirement in 2004 as Superintendent of Schools in suburban Ringwood, New Jersey. Mr. Carter enjoyed to the fullest each one of his positions as he traveled across New York, Delaware, and New Jersey enriching the lives of the K-12 student population.

During his 36+ year career, Carter was the recipient of numerous awards for distinguished service in his chosen field as a school educational leader. Though retiring in 2004, he continued to be called upon to lend his expertise in education in Interim Superintendent roles, volunteering in the local elementary schools, and serving as an expert witness/consultant for several New Jersey law firms. Peter had also been busy serving in local leadership positions, which included two homeowner association boards and the board of the Delaware Botanic Gardens.

His passion for literature and writing continued to be enhanced by his published articles in his local Rehoboth Beach, Delaware newspaper, his 2020 autobiography- A BLACK FIRST, and his 2021 sequel - A BLACK FIRST: The Blackness Continues… where he shared the trials and tribulations of his 36-year working career and retirement life in education. Being the "first" in many situations, both books allow you to experience his journey of weathering the storms of racism and bigotry and applaud his victories as he overcomes those obstacles. Done all for one purpose, to give children the best education possible.

Mr. Carter passed away on May 8, 2023. He is survived by his two children, two grandchildren, and many friends, students, staff, and formal and informal mentees.